SEQUENTIAL
CHRISTMAS PIANO SONGS

ISBN 978-1-5400-5459-3

Visit Hal Leonard Online at
www.halleonard.com

Contact us:
Hal Leonard
7777 West Bluemound Road
Milwaukee, WI 53213
Email: info@halleonard.com

In Europe, contact:
Hal Leonard Europe Limited
42 Wigmore Street
Marylebone, London, W1U 2RN
Email: info@halleonardeurope.com

In Australia, contact:
Hal Leonard Australia Pty. Ltd.
4 Lentara Court
Cheltenham, Victoria, 3192 Australia
Email: info@halleonard.com.au

The 26 songs in this book are presented in a basic order of difficulty, beginning with the easiest arrangements (hands alone, very simple rhythms) and progressing to more difficult arrangements including hands together, syncopated rhythms, chromatic harmony, and moving around the keyboard.

THE CHIPMUNK SONG

Words and Music by
ROSS BAGDASARIAN

Happily

Christ - mas, Christ - mas time is near,

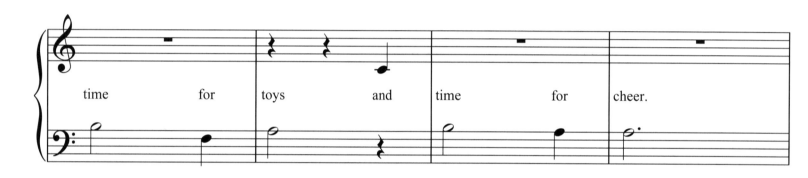

time for toys and time for cheer.

We've been good, but we can't last,

hur - y, Christ - mas, hur - ry fast!

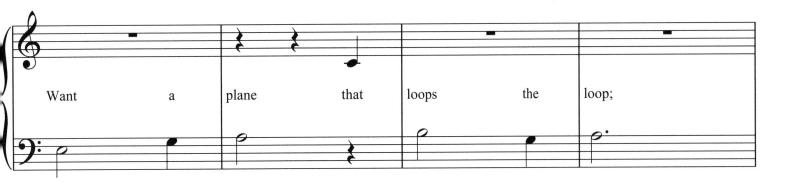

Want a plane that loops the loop;

me, I want a hu - la hoop.

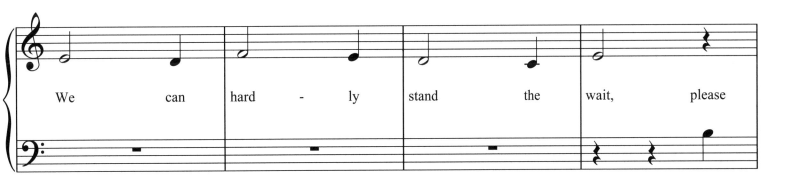

We can hard - ly stand the wait, please

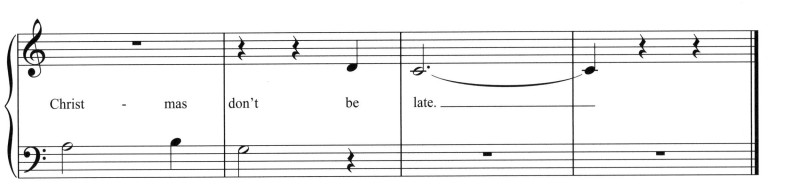

Christ - mas don't be late. _____

WHITE CHRISTMAS
from the Motion Picture Irving Berlin's HOLIDAY INN

Words and Music by
IRVING BERLIN

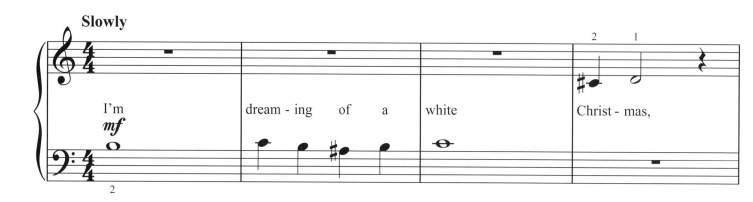

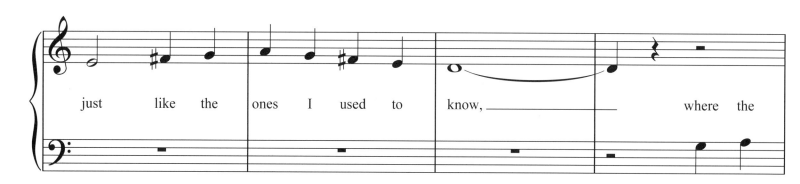

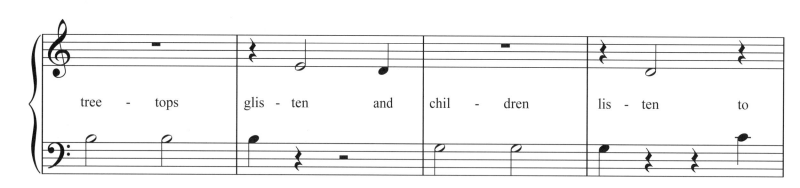

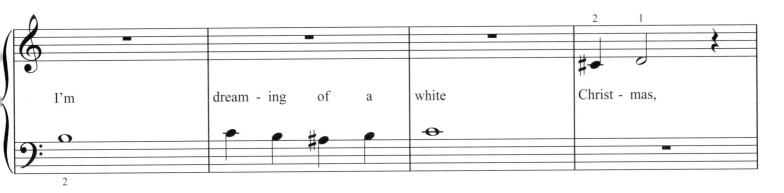

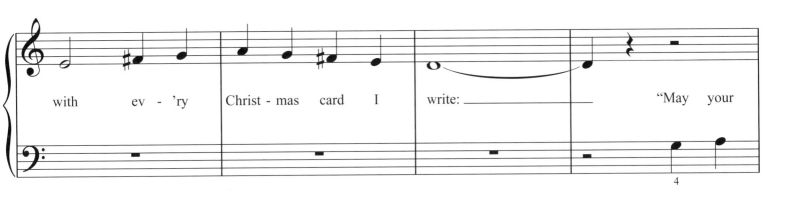

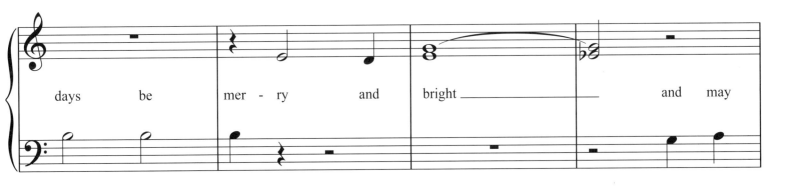

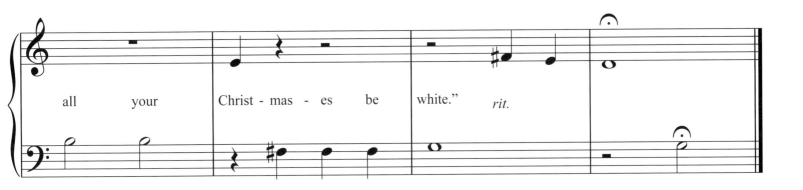

ALL I WANT FOR CHRISTMAS IS MY TWO FRONT TEETH

Words and Music by
DON GARDNER

Moderately

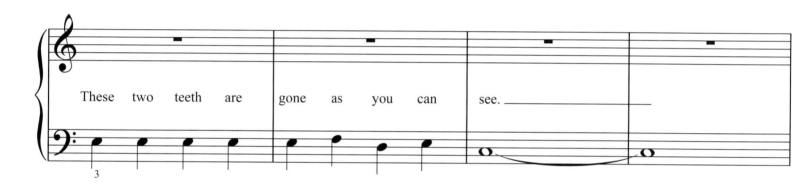

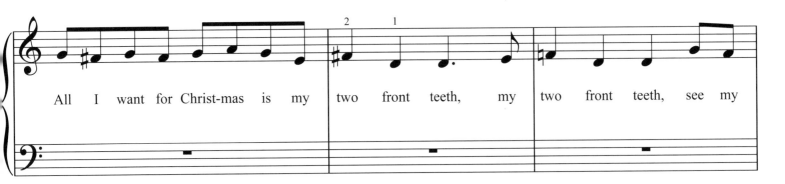

All I want for Christ-mas is my two front teeth, my two front teeth, see my

two front teeth! Gee, if I could on - ly have my two front teeth, then

I could wish you "Mer - ry Christ - mas!" It seems so long since

I could say, "Sis - ter Su - sie sit - ting on a this - tle!"

Gosh, oh gee, how hap - py I'd be, if I could on - ly

whis - tle. All I want for Christ-mas is my two front teeth, my

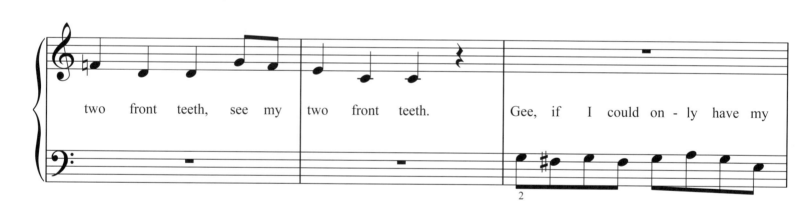

two front teeth, see my two front teeth. Gee, if I could on - ly have my

two front teeth, then I could wish you "Mer - ry Christ - mas!"

HERE COMES SANTA CLAUS
(Right Down Santa Claus Lane)

Words and Music by GENE AUTRY
and OAKLEY HALDEMAN

Moderately bright

Here comes San-ta Claus! Here comes San-ta Claus! Right down San-ta Claus Lane!

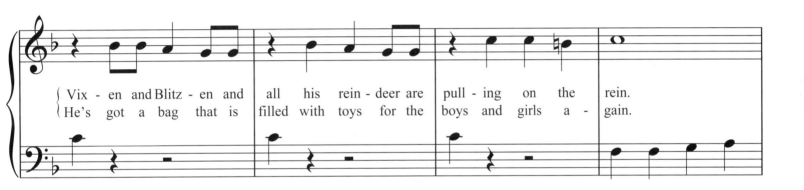

Vix - en and Blitz - en and all his rein-deer are pull - ing on the rein.
He's got a bag that is filled with toys for the boys and girls a - gain.

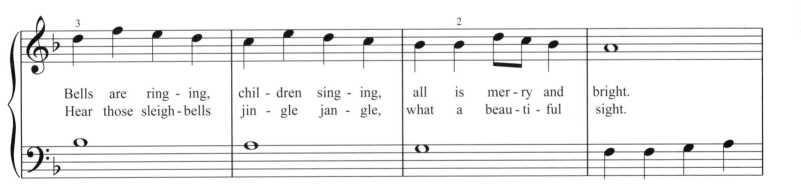

Bells are ring - ing, chil - dren sing - ing, all is mer - ry and bright.
Hear those sleigh-bells jin - gle jan - gle, what a beau - ti - ful sight.

Hang your stock-ings and say your pray'rs, 'cause San-ta Claus comes to - night. night.
Jump in bed, cov - er up your head,

BLUE CHRISTMAS

Words and Music by BILLY HAYES
and JAY JOHNSON

Moderately, in 2

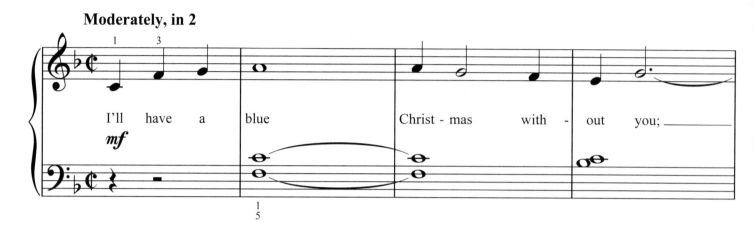

I'll have a   blue   Christ - mas   with - out   you; _____

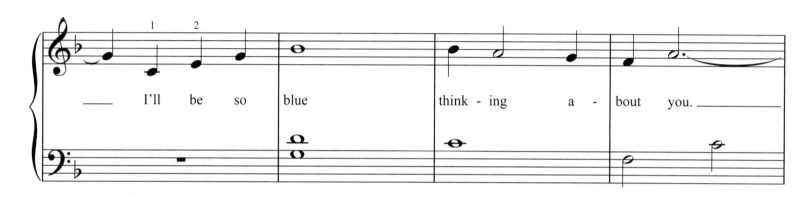

_____ I'll   be   so   blue   think - ing   a - bout   you. _____

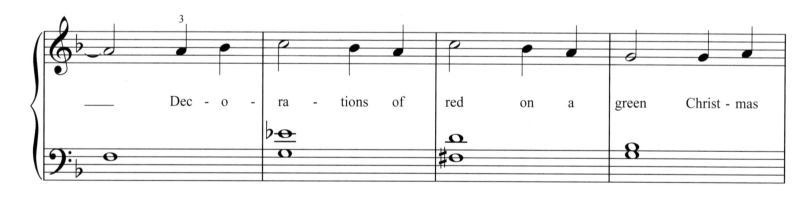

_____ Dec - o - ra - tions of   red   on a   green   Christ - mas

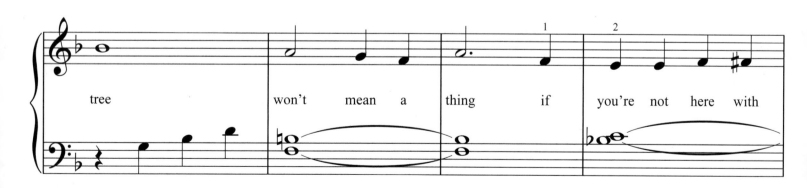

tree   won't   mean   a   thing   if   you're   not   here   with

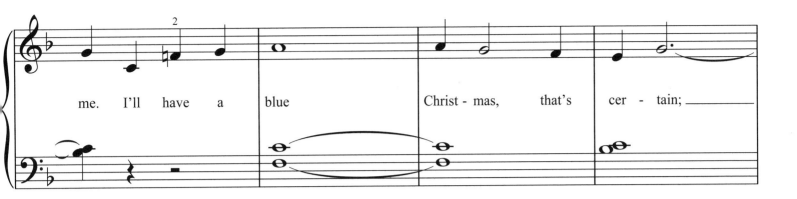

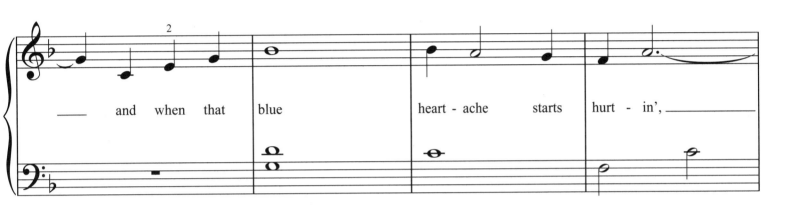

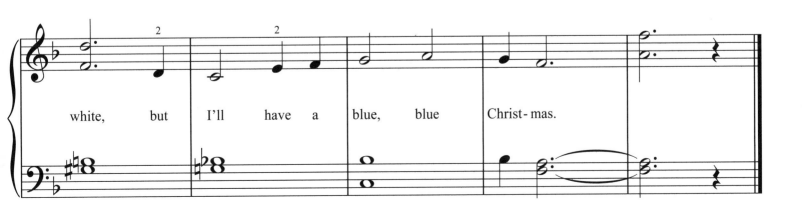

I'LL BE HOME FOR CHRISTMAS

Words and Music by KIM GANNON
and WALTER KENT

Moderately

I'll   be   home   for   Christ - mas. _____

You   can   count   on   me.

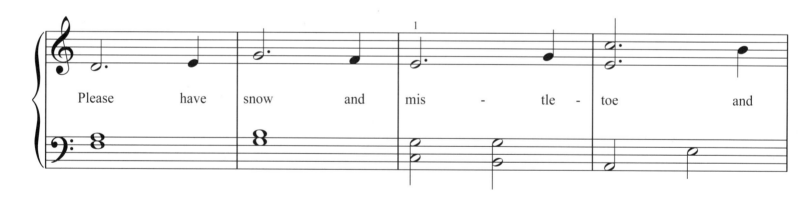

Please   have   snow   and   mis - tle - toe   and

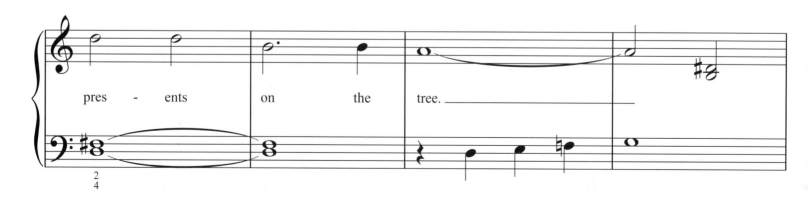

pres - ents   on   the   tree. _____

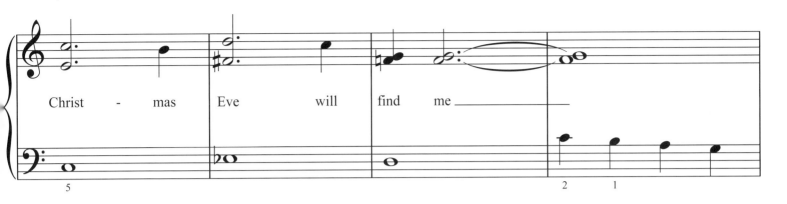

Christ - mas Eve will find me

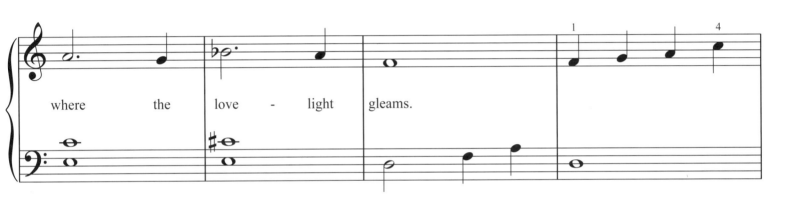

where the love - light gleams.

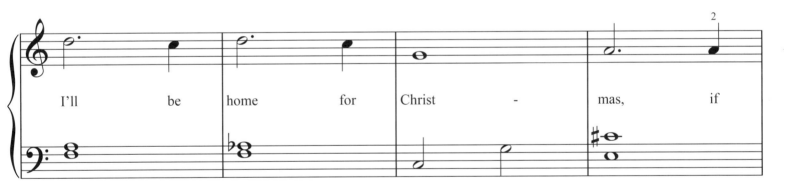

I'll be home for Christ - mas, if

on - ly in my dreams. *rit.*

A CHILD IS BORN

Music by THAD JONES
Lyrics by ALEC WILDER

Slow Jazz Ballad

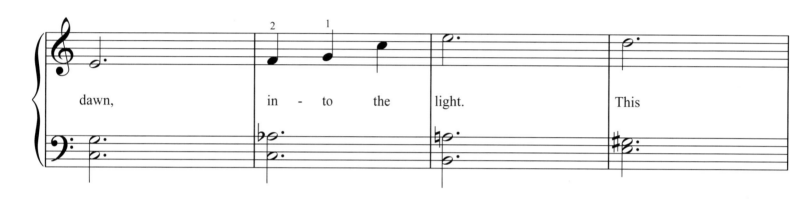

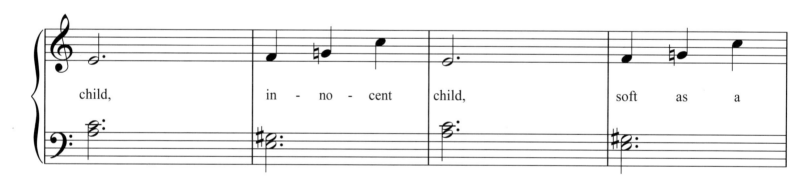

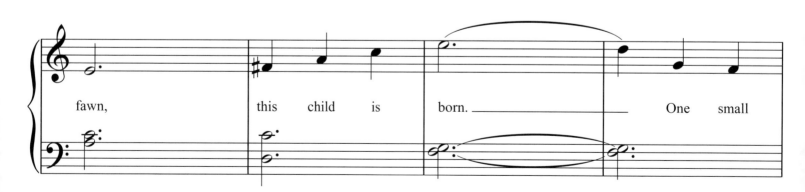

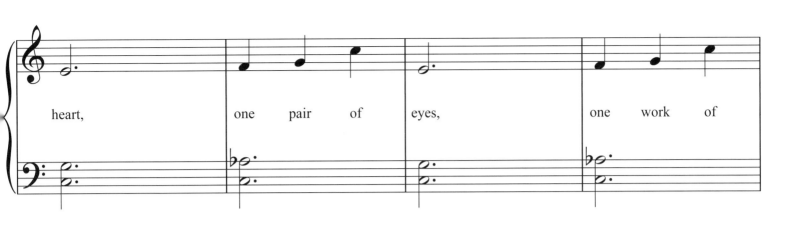

heart,   one   pair   of   eyes,   one   work   of

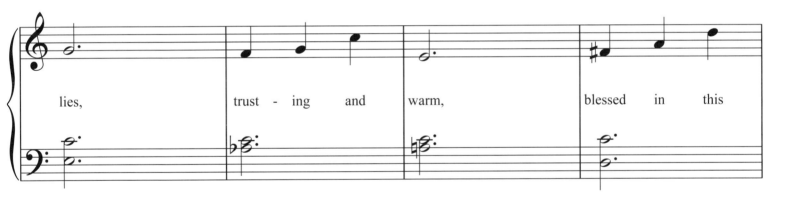

art   here   in   my   arms._____   Here   he

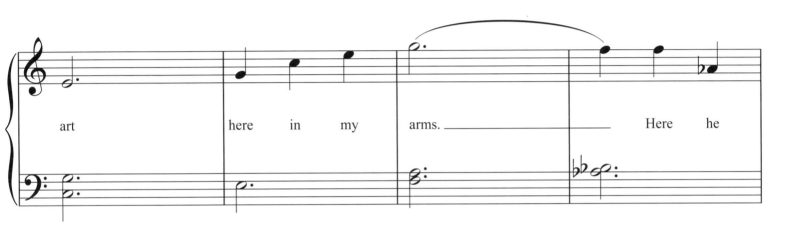

lies,   trust - ing   and   warm,   blessed   in   this

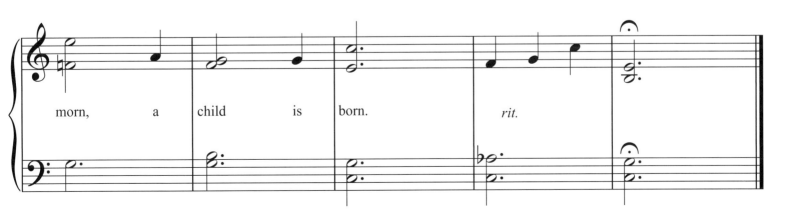

morn,   a   child   is   born.   *rit.*

LET IT SNOW! LET IT SNOW! LET IT SNOW!

Words by SAMMY CAHN
Music by JULE STYNE

Moderately, in 2

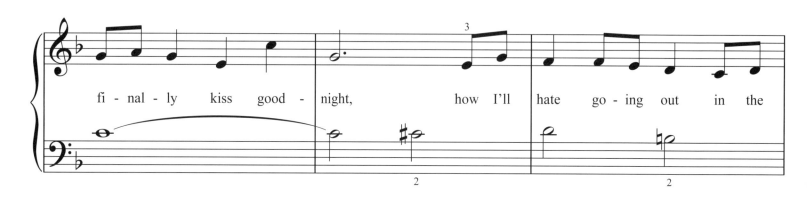

storm; but if you'll real - ly hold me tight,

all the way home I'll be warm. The fire is slow - ly

dy - ing, and my dear, we're still good - bye - ing, but as

long as you love me so, let it snow, let it snow, let it snow.

DO YOU HEAR WHAT I HEAR

Words and Music by NOEL REGNEY
and GLORIA SHAYNE

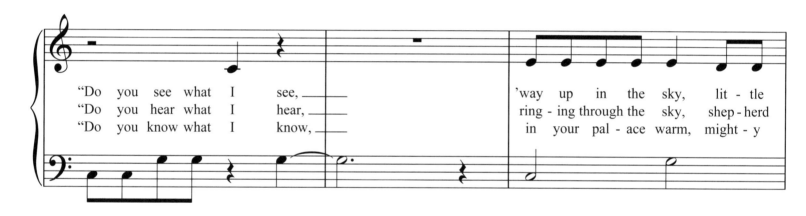

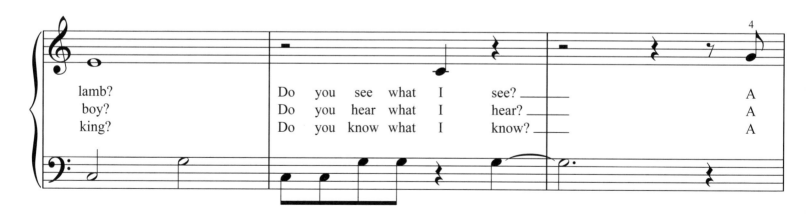

star, a star, danc - ing in the night, with a tail as big as a
song, a song, high a - bove the tree, with a voice as big as the
Child, a Child shiv - ers in the cold; let us bring Him sil - ver and

kite, with a tail as big as a kite."
sea, with a voice as big as the sea."
gold, let us bring Him sil - ver and gold."

1., 2.   3.

_____   Said the _____   Said the king to the peo - ple ev - 'ry
_____   Said the

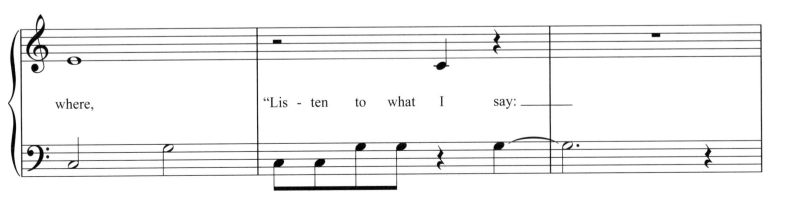

where,   "Lis - ten to what I say:

Pray for peace, peo - ple ev - 'ry - where!

Lis - ten to what I say: ____

____ The Child, the Child sleep - ing in the night, He will

bring us good - ness and light, He will bring us good - ness and

light!

THE MOST WONDERFUL TIME OF THE YEAR

Words and Music by EDDIE POLA
and GEORGE WYLE

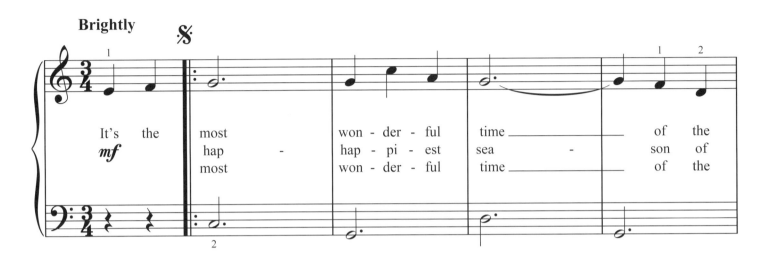

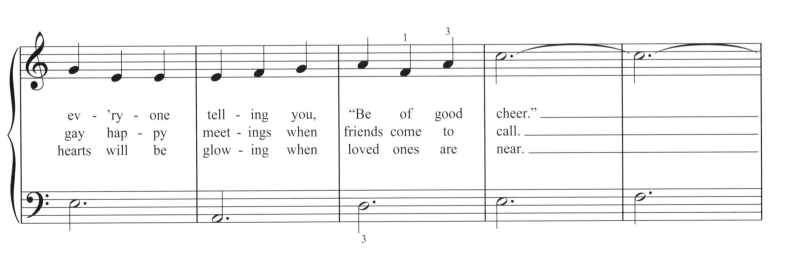

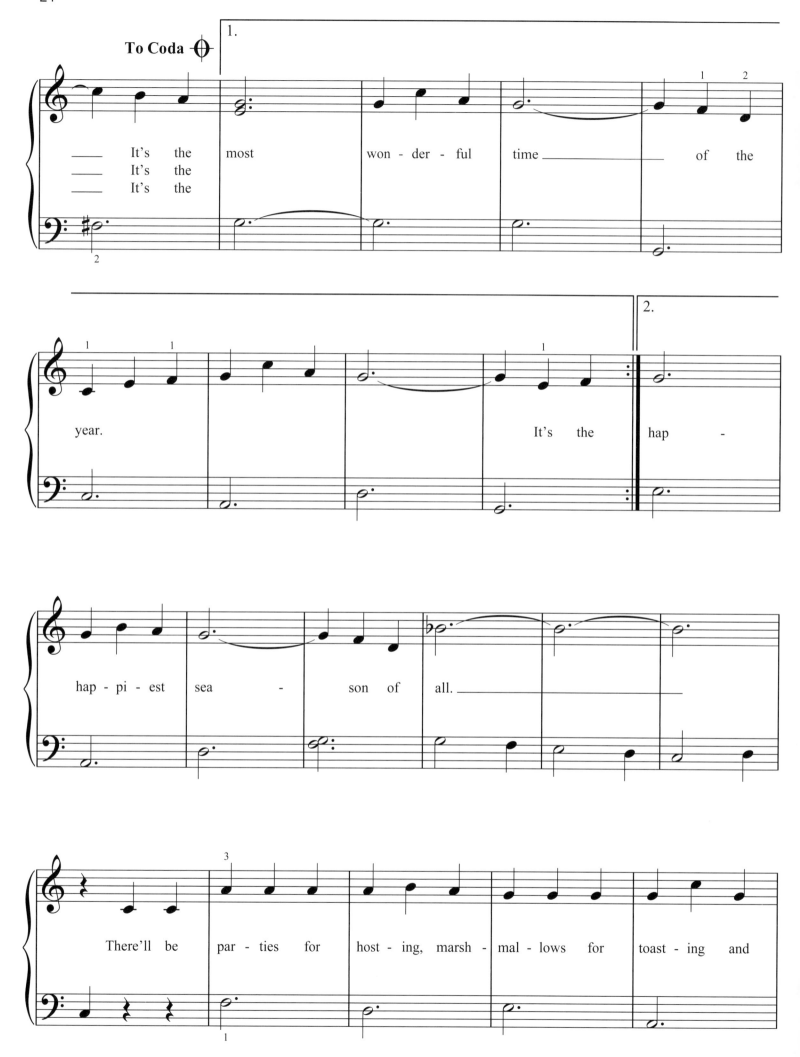

car - ol - ing out in the snow. _____ There'll be scar - y ghost

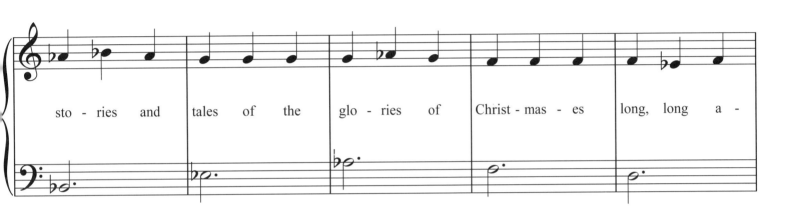

sto - ries and tales of the glo - ries of Christ - mas - es long, long a -

D.S. al Coda

go. _____ It's the

CODA

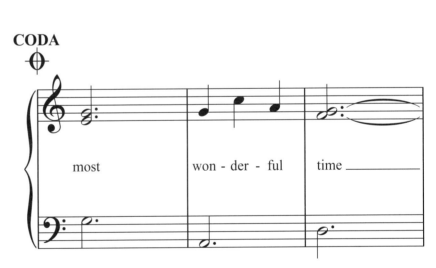

most won - der - ful time _____

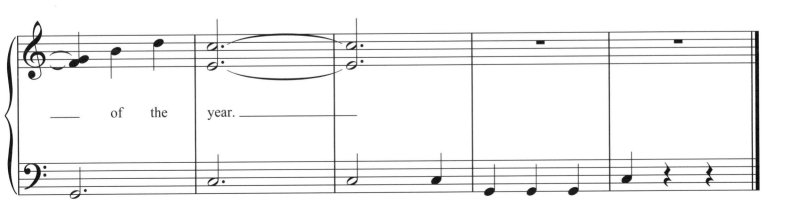

_____ of the year. _____

HAVE YOURSELF A MERRY LITTLE CHRISTMAS

from MEET ME IN ST. LOUIS

Words and Music by HUGH MARTIN
and RALPH BLANE

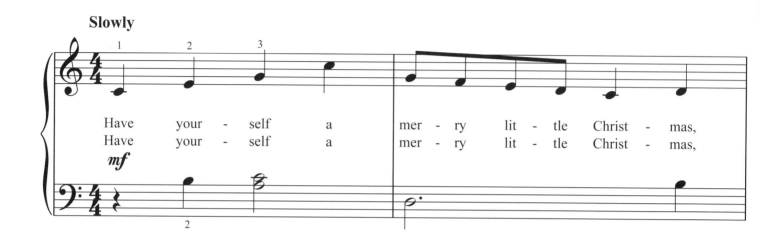

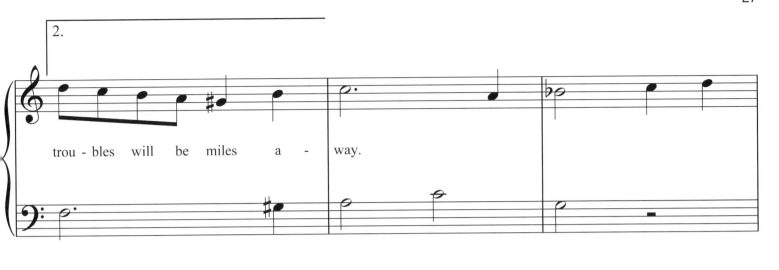

2.

trou - bles will be miles a - way.

Here we are as in old - en days, hap - py

gold - en days of yore. Faith - ful friends who are

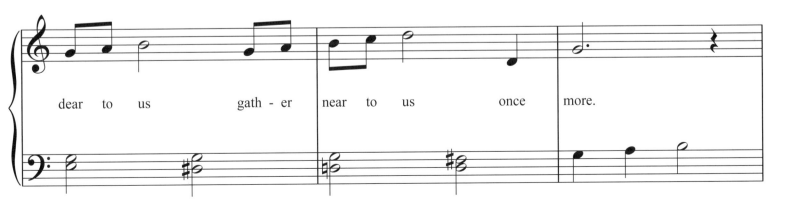

dear to us gath - er near to us once more.

Through the years we all will be to-geth-er, if the Fates al-

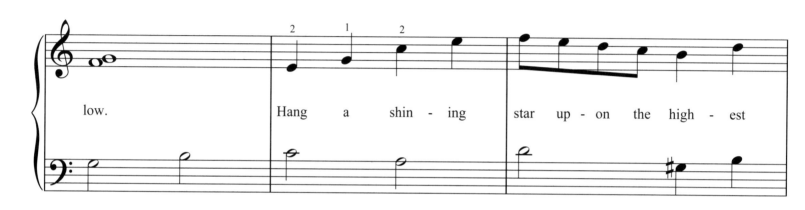

low. Hang a shin-ing star up-on the high-est

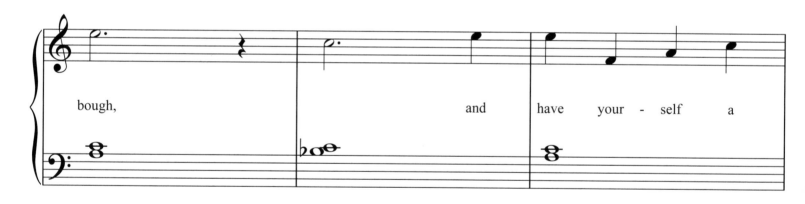

bough, and have your-self a

mer-ry lit-tle Christ-mas now. *rit.*

BELIEVE

from Warner Bros. Pictures' THE POLAR EXPRESS

Words and Music by GLEN BALLARD
and ALAN SILVESTRI

Moderately slow

Chil - dren sleep - ing,
Trains move quick - ly

snow is soft - ly
to their jour - ney's

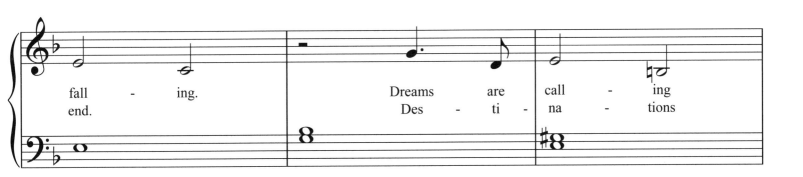

fall - ing.
end.

Dreams are call - ing
Des - ti - na - tions

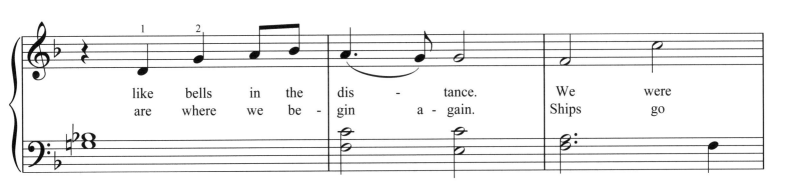

like bells in the dis - tance. We were
are where we be - gin a - gain. Ships go

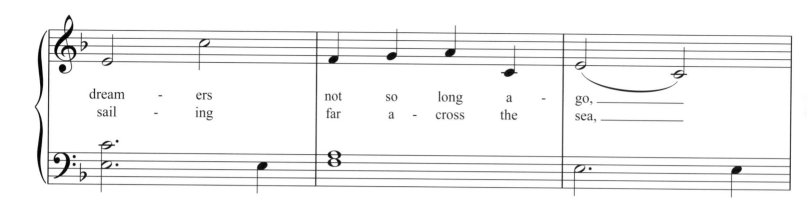

dream - ers not so long a - go, _____
sail - ing far a - cross the sea, _____

but one by one, we   all had to
trust - ing star - light   to get where they

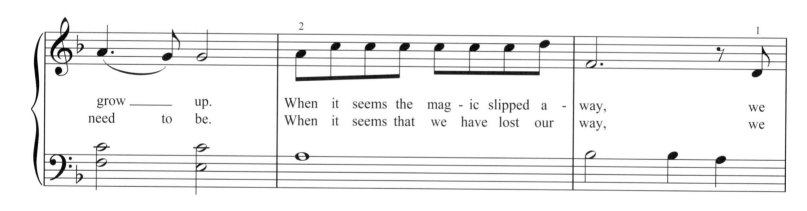

grow _____ up. When it seems the mag - ic slipped a - way, we
need to be. When it seems that we have lost our way, we

find it all a - gain on Christ - mas Day.
find our-selves a - gain on Christ - mas Day.   Be - lieve in what your heart is say - ing,

hear the mel - o - dy that's play - ing. There's no time to waste, there's so much to cel - e - brate. Be -

lieve in what you feel in - side and give your dreams the wings to fly.

1.

You have ev - 'ry-thing you need if you just ____ be - lieve.

2.

____ be - lieve. *rit.*

THE CHRISTMAS SONG
(Chestnuts Roasting on an Open Fire)

Music and Lyric by MEL TORMÉ
and ROBERT WELLS

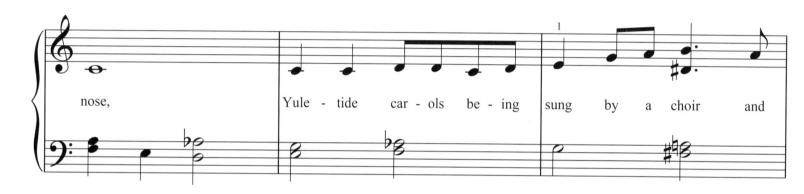

bright.　　Ti - ny tots with their eyes all a - glow will

find it hard to sleep to - night.　　They know that San - ta's on his

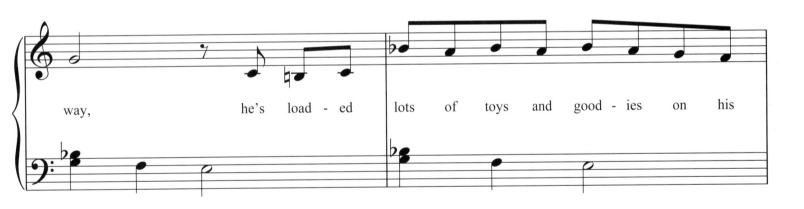

way,　　he's load - ed lots of toys and good - ies on his

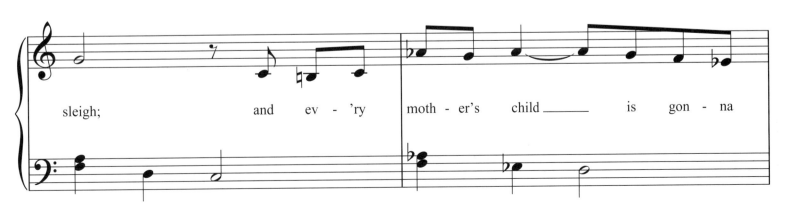

sleigh;　　and ev - 'ry moth - er's child ____ is gon - na

spy _____ to see if rein - deer real - ly know how to

fly. And so, I'm of - fer - ing this sim - ple phrase ___ to

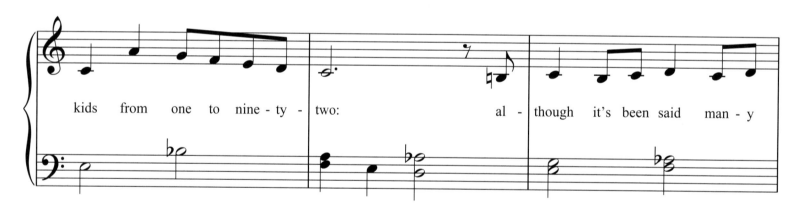

kids from one to nine - ty - two: al - though it's been said man - y

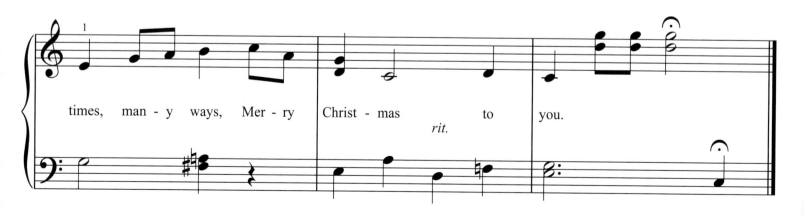

times, man - y ways, Mer - ry Christ - mas to you.

rit.

A HOLLY JOLLY CHRISTMAS

Music and Lyrics by
JOHNNY MARKS

Merrily

Have a hol - ly jol - ly Christ - mas, it's the

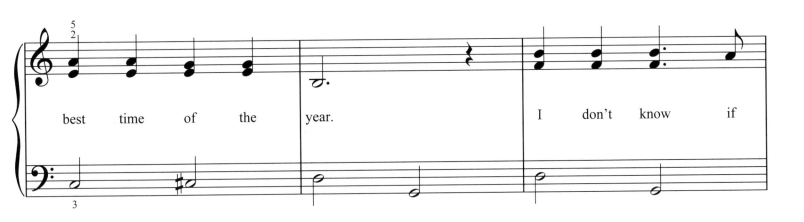

best time of the year. I don't know if

there'll be snow, but let's all give a cheer. Have a

hol - ly jol - ly Christ - mas and when you walk down the

street, say hel - lo to friends you know and

ev - 'ry - one you meet. Oh, ho, the

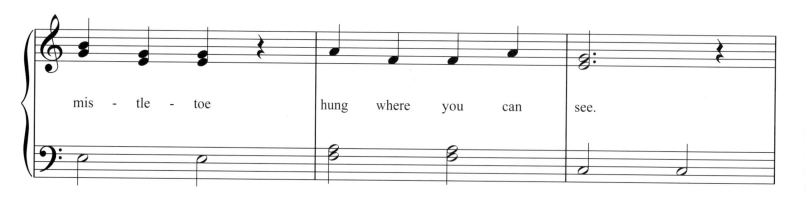

mis - tle - toe hung where you can see.

Some - bod - y waits for you, kiss her once for

me. Have a hol - ly jol - ly Christ - mas and in

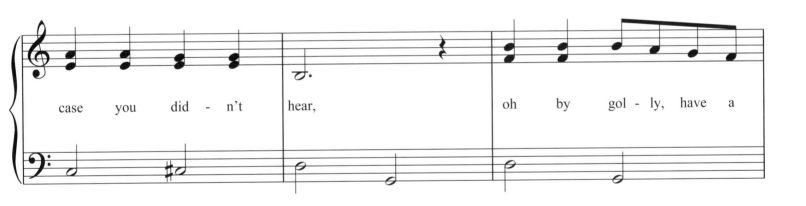

case you did - n't hear, oh by gol - ly, have a

hol - ly jol - ly Christ - mas this year.

SANTA CLAUS IS COMIN' TO TOWN

Words by HAVEN GILLESPIE
Music by J. FRED COOTS

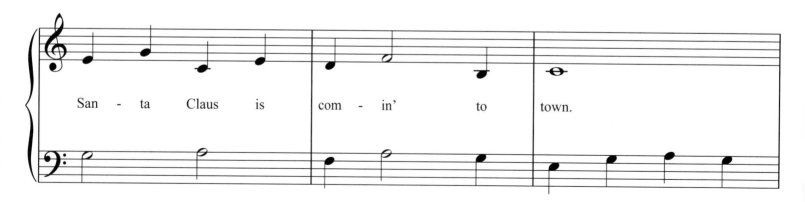

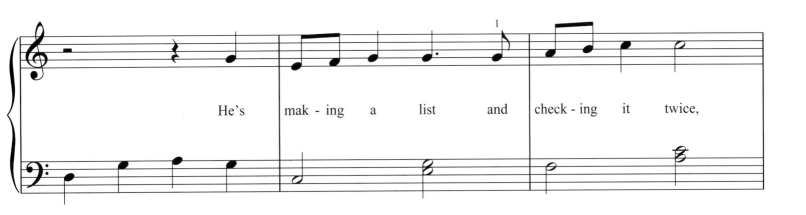

He's mak - ing a list and check - ing it twice,

gon - na find out who's naugh - ty and nice, San - ta Claus is

com - in' to town. He

sees you when you're sleep - in', he knows when you're a -

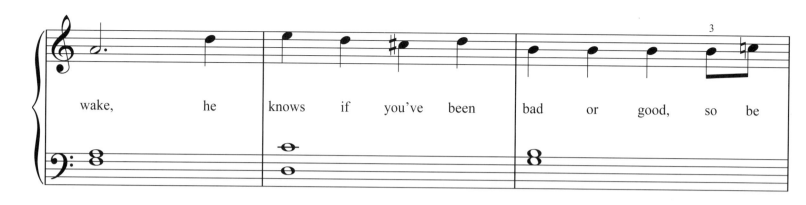

wake, he knows if you've been bad or good, so be

good for good - ness' sake. You bet - ter watch out, you

bet - ter not cry, bet - ter not pout, I'm tell - ing you why:

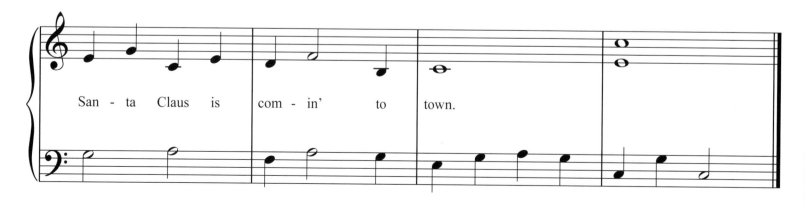

San - ta Claus is com - in' to town.

WINTER WONDERLAND

Words by DICK SMITH
Music by FELIX BERNARD

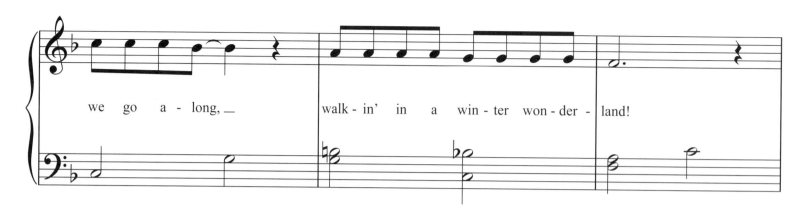

we go a-long, ___ walk-in' in a win-ter won-der-land!

In the mead-ow we can build a snow-man, then pre-tend that he is Par-son
In the mead-ow we can build a snow-man, and pre-tend that he's a cir-cus

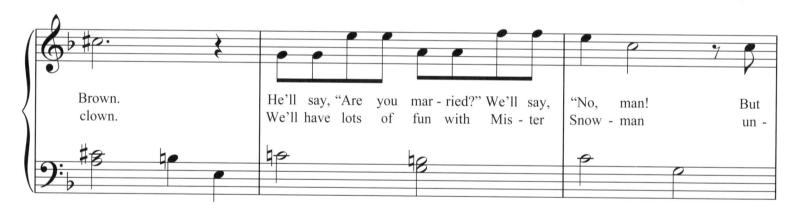

Brown.
clown.
He'll say, "Are you mar-ried?" We'll say, "No, man! But
We'll have lots of fun with Mis-ter Snow-man un-

you can do the job when you're in town!" Lat-er on, we'll con-
til the oth-er kid-dies knock him down! When it snows, it's so

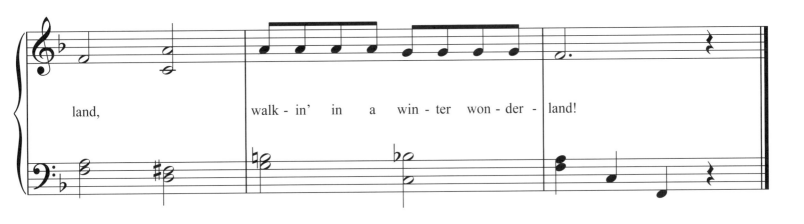

FROSTY THE SNOW MAN

Words and Music by STEVE NELSON
and JACK ROLLINS

Frost - y   the   Snow   Man   was   a
Frost - y   the   Snow   Man   knew   the

jol - ly hap - py   soul,   with a   corn - cob   pipe   and a
sun was   hot that day.   So he   said, "Let's   run   and we'll

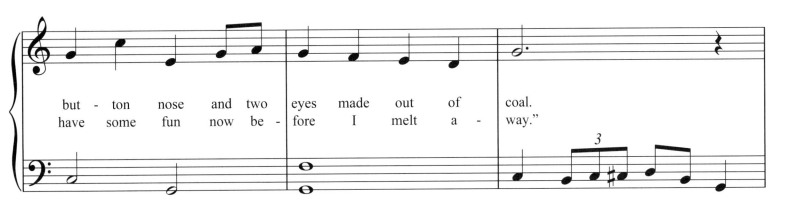

but - ton nose and two eyes made out of coal.
have some fun now be - fore I melt a - way."

Frost - y the Snow Man is a fair - y tale they
Down to the vil - lage with a broom - stick in his

say; he was made of snow, but the chil - dren know how he
hand, run - ning here and there all a - round the square, say - in',

came to life one day. There must have been some
"Catch me if you can." He led them down the

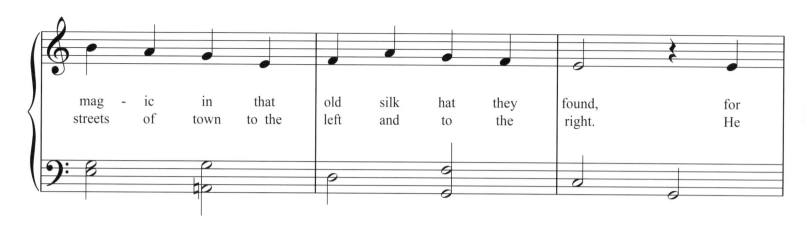

mag - ic in that old silk hat they found, for
streets of town to the left and to they the right. He

when they placed it on his head, he be - gan to dance a -
ran so placed fast he dis - ap - peared, yep, he was out of

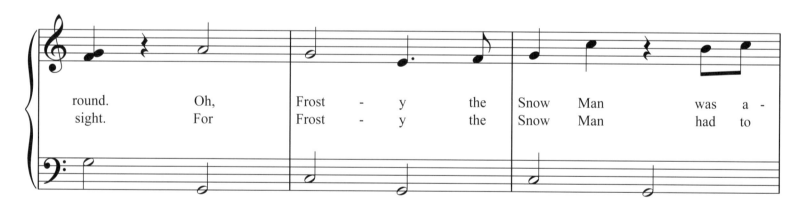

round. Oh, Frost - y the Snow Man was a -
sight. For Frost - y the Snow Man had to

live as he could be, and the chil - dren say he could
hur - ry on his way, but he waved good - bye, say - in',

JINGLE BELL ROCK

Words and Music by JOE BEAL
and JIM BOOTHE

Jin - gle bell, jin - gle bell, jin - gle bell rock, ___
Jin - gle bell, jin - gle bell, jin - gle bell rock, ___

jin - gle bell swing ___ and jin - gle bells ring. ___
jin - gle bell chime ___ in jin - gle bell time, ___

Snow - in' and blow - in' up bush - els of fun; ___
danc - in' and pranc - in' in Jin - gle Bell Square ___

now the jin - gle hop has be - gun. __ | in the frost - y

air. What a bright time, __ it's the right time __ to

rock the night a - way. Jin - gle bell time __ is a

swell time __ to go glid - in' in a one-horse sleigh. __

Gid - dy - ap, jin - gle horse, pick up your feet, ____

jin - gle a - round the clock. Mix and min - gle in a

jin - gl - in' beat, __ that's the jin - gle bell, that's the jin - gle bell,

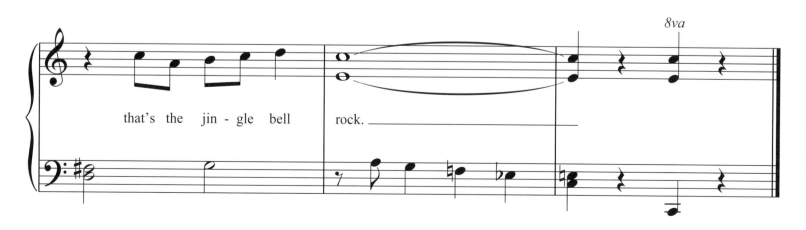

that's the jin - gle bell rock. ____

RUDOLPH THE RED-NOSED REINDEER

Music and Lyrics by
JOHNNY MARKS

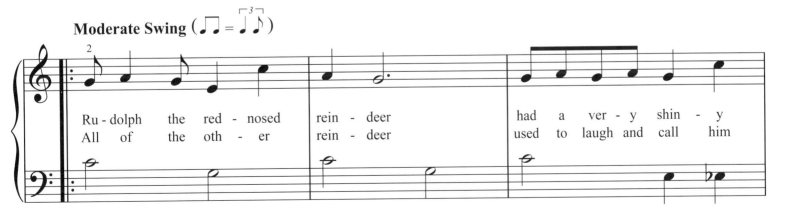

nose,
and if you ev - er saw it, you would e - ven say it
names.
They nev - er let poor Ru - dolph

glows.
join in an - y rein - deer games.

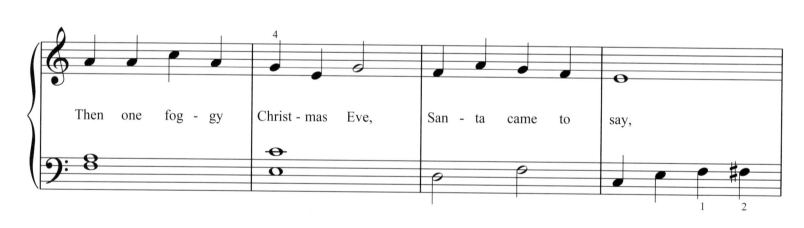

Then one fog - gy Christ - mas Eve, San - ta came to say,

"Ru - dolph with your nose so bright, won't you guide my sleigh to - night?"

Then how the rein - deer loved him, as they shout - ed out with

glee, "Ru - dolph the red - nosed rein - deer,

you'll go down in his - to - ry!" You'll go down in his - to -

ry! _____

A MARSHMALLOW WORLD

Words by CARL SIGMAN
Music by PETER DE ROSE

It's a marsh-mal-low world in the win-ter _____ when the snow comes to cov-er the
marsh-mal-low clouds be-ing friend-ly _____ in the arms of the ev-er-green

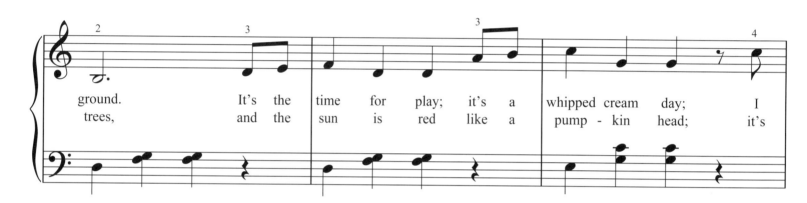

ground. It's the time for play; it's a whipped cream day; I
trees, and the sun is red like a pump-kin head; it's

wait for it the whole year 'round. Those are shin-ing so your nose won't

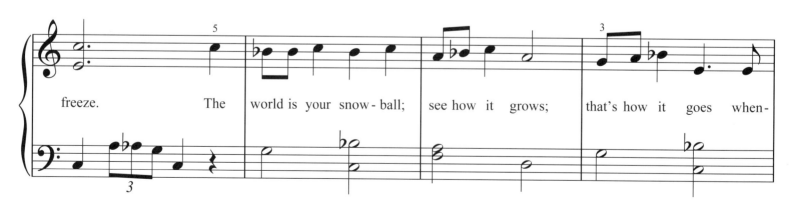

freeze. The world is your snow-ball; see how it grows; that's how it goes when-

ev - er it snows. The world is your snow - ball; just for a song, get out and roll it a -

long. It's a yum, yum - my world made for sweet - hearts; take a

walk with your fa - vor - ite girl. It's a sug - ar date; what if

spring is late? In win - ter, it's a marsh - mal - low world.

8vb

I WONDER AS I WANDER

By JOHN JACOB NILES

under the sky. When | Mar - y birthed Je - sus, 'twas | in a cow's stall, with
He was the King. I | won - der as I wan - der, out | un - der the sky, how

wise men and farm - ers and | shep - herds and all. But | high from God's heav - en a
Je - sus the Sav - ior did | come for to die But | for poor on - 'ry peo - ple like

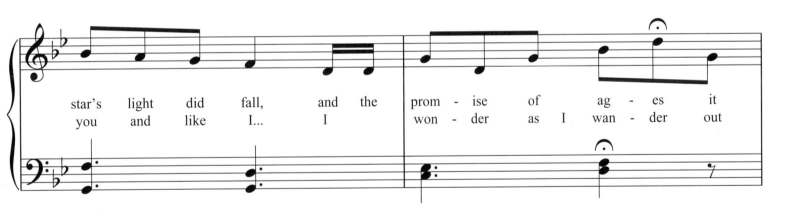

star's light did fall, and the | prom - ise of ag - es it
you and like I... I | won - der as I wan - der out

1.
then did re - call. If

2.
un - der the sky.

MARY, DID YOU KNOW?

Words and Music by MARK LOWRY
and BUDDY GREENE

Slowly, in 2

Mar-y, did you

know   that your ba - by boy __ would one day walk __ on
know   that your ba - by boy __ will give sight to __ a
know   that your ba - by boy __ is Lord of all __ cre -

wa - ter? Mar-y, did you know   that your ba - by boy __ would
blind man? Mar-y, did you know   that your ba - by boy __ would
a - tion? Mar-y, did you know   that your ba - by boy __ will

save our sons __ and daugh - ters? Did you know __ that your ba -
calm a storm __ with His hand? Did you know __ that your ba -
one day rule __ the na - tions? Did you know __ that your ba -

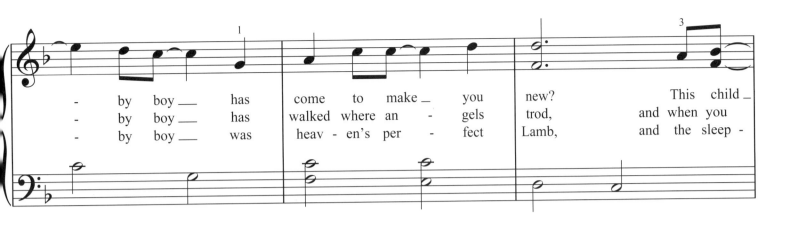

- by boy ___ has come to make ___ you new? This child ___
- by boy ___ has walked where an - gels trod, and when you
- by boy ___ was heav - en's per - fect Lamb, and the sleep -

To Coda ⊕

___ that you ___ de - liv - ered will soon de - liv - er
kissed your lit - tle ba - by, you've kissed the face ___ of
- ing Child ___ you're

1.

2.

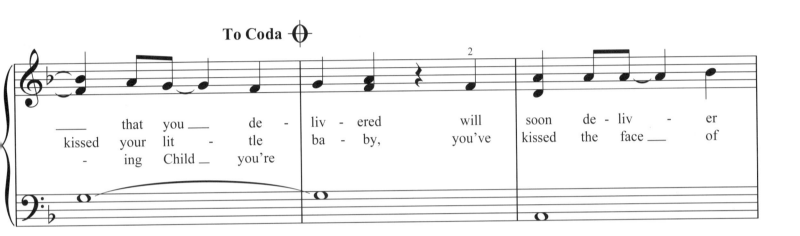

you. Mar - y, did you God? Oh, Mar - y did you know?

The blind will see, ___ the

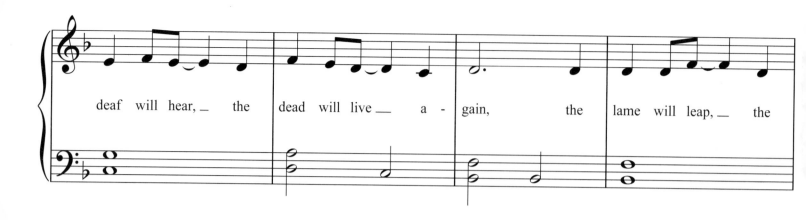

deaf will hear, __ the dead will live __ a - gain, the lame will leap, __ the

D.S. al Coda

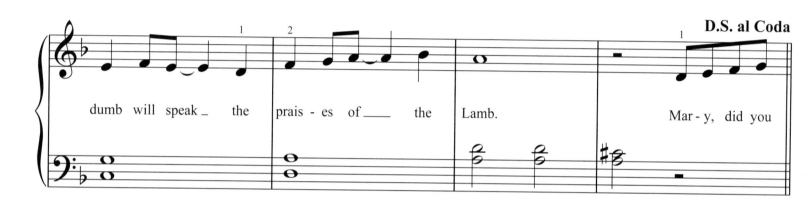

dumb will speak __ the prais - es of ___ the Lamb. Mar - y, did you

CODA

hold - ing is the great I AM?

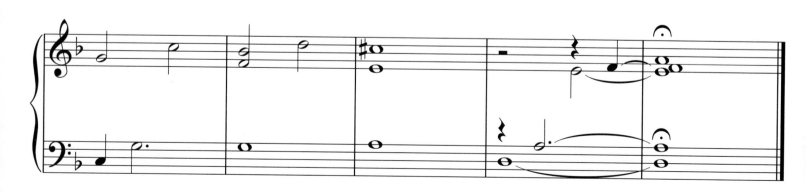

COVENTRY CAROL

Words by ROBERT CROO
Traditional English Melody

FELIZ NAVIDAD

Music and Lyrics by
JOSÉ FELICIANO

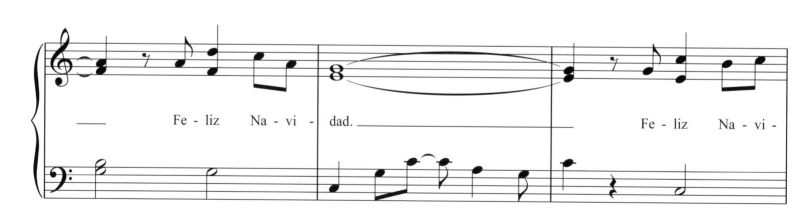

heart. _____

I want to wish you a Mer - ry Christ-mas

with mis - tle - toe and __ lots of cheer, __

with lots of laugh - ter through-

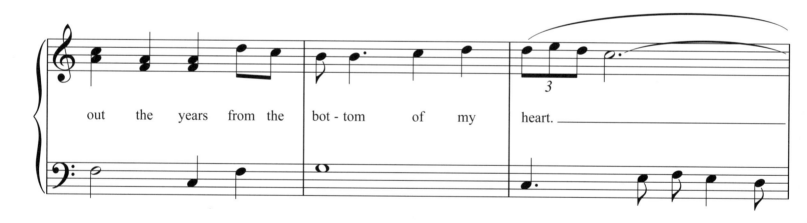

out the years from the bot - tom of my heart. _____

D.S. al Coda

_____ Fe - liz Na - vi -

CODA

SOMEWHERE IN MY MEMORY

from the Twentieth Century Fox Motion Picture HOME ALONE

Words by LESLIE BRICUSSE
Music by JOHN WILLIAMS

Gently, with simplicity

Can - dles in the win - dow, shad - ows paint - ing the

ceil - ing, gaz - ing at the fire glow,

feel - ing that "gin - ger - bread" feel - ing. Pre - cious mo - ments,

spe - cial peo - ple, hap - py fac - es I can see.

Some - where in my mem - 'ry, Christ - mas joys all a -

round me, liv - ing in my mem - 'ry,

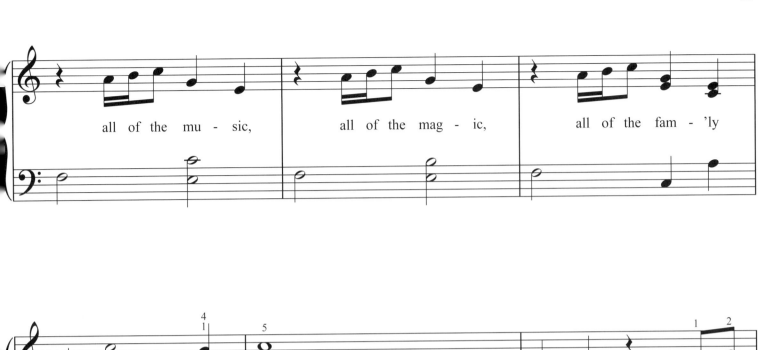

all of the mu - sic, all of the mag - ic, all of the fam - 'ly

home here   with   me.

IT'S BEGINNING TO LOOK LIKE CHRISTMAS

By MEREDITH WILLSON

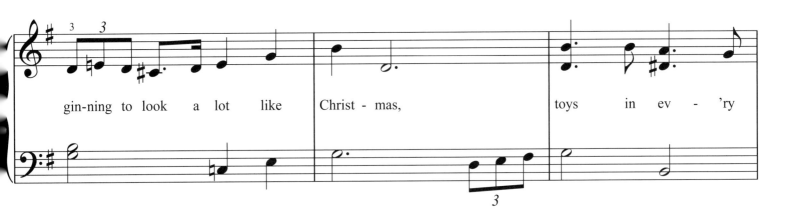

gin-ning to look a lot like Christ - mas, toys in ev - 'ry

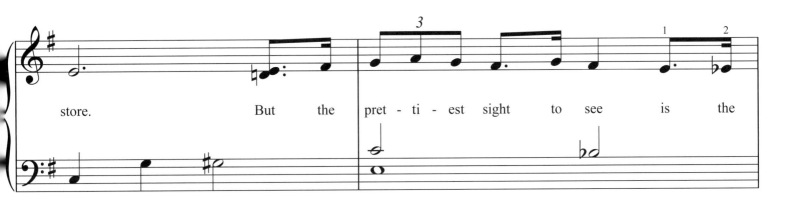

store. But the pret - ti - est sight to see is the

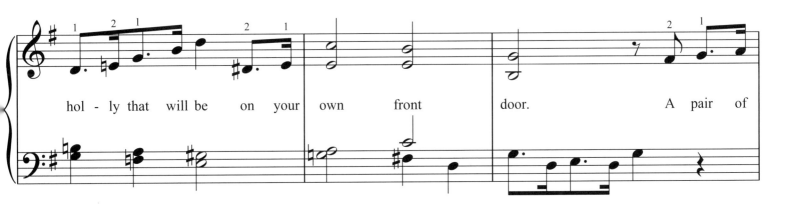

hol - ly that will be on your own front door. A pair of

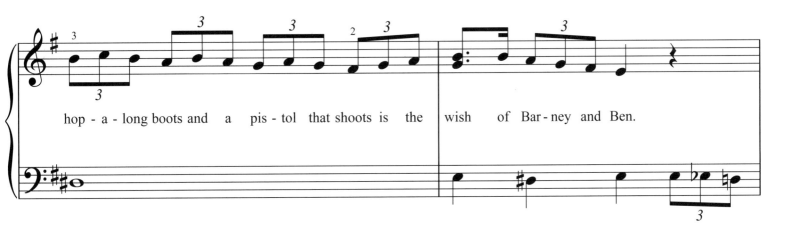

hop - a - long boots and a pis - tol that shoots is the wish of Bar - ney and Ben.

70

Dolls that will talk and will go for a walk is the hope of Jan-ice and Jen. And

Mom and Dad can hard - ly wait for school to start a - gain. It's be -

gin - ning to look a lot like Christ - mas,

ev - 'ry - where you go. There's a tree in the Grand Ho - tel,

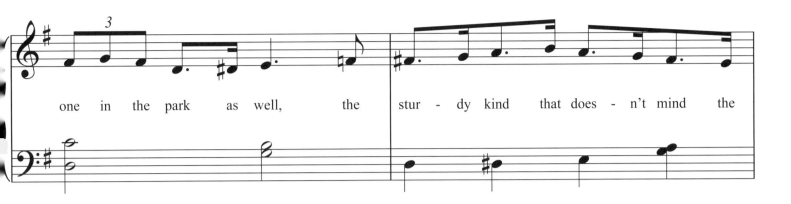

one in the park as well, the stur - dy kind that does - n't mind the

snow. It's be - gin-ning to look a lot like Christ - mas,

soon the bells will start. And the thing that will make them ring is the

car - ol that you sing right with - in your heart.

SEQUENTIAL
PIANO SONGBOOK SERIES

Pianists of all levels can enjoy current and classic hits with *Sequential Piano Songs!* Starting with the easiest arrangements (hands alone, very simple rhythms) and progressing in order of difficulty (hands together, syncopated rhythms and moving around the keyboard), these supplemental songbooks are a terrific resource for improving music reading and piano skills from the very first page.

SEQUENTIAL CHRISTMAS PIANO SONGS

26 Holiday Favorites Carefully Selected and Arranged in Order of Difficulty

All I Want for Christmas Is My Two Front Teeth • Believe • The Christmas Song (Chestnuts Roasting on an Open Fire) • Frosty the Snow Man • It's Beginning to Look like Christmas • Jingle Bell Rock • Mary, Did You Know? • Rudolph the Red-Nosed Reindeer • White Christmas • and more.

00294929 Easy Piano..................................$16.99

SEQUENTIAL DISNEY PIANO SONGS

24 Easy Favorites Carefully Selected and Arranged in Order of Difficulty

Be Our Guest • Can You Feel the Love Tonight • Chim Chim Cher-ee • A Dream Is a Wish Your Heart Makes • Evermore • I See the Light • Kiss the Girl • Let It Go • A Whole New World (Aladdin's Theme) • The World Es Mi Familia • You've Got a Friend in Me • and more.

00294870 Easy Piano..................................$16.99

SEQUENTIAL JAZZ PIANO SONGS

26 Easy Favorites Carefully Selected and Arranged in Order of Difficulty

All the Things You Are • Autumn Leaves • Bye Bye Blackbird • Fly Me to the Moon (In Other Words) • I Got Rhythm • It Could Happen to You • Misty • My Funny Valentine • Satin Doll • Stardust • Take Five • The Way You Look Tonight • When I Fall in Love • and more.

00286967 Easy Piano..................................$16.99

SEQUENTIAL KIDS' PIANO SONGS

24 Easy Favorites Carefully Selected and Arranged in Order of Difficulty

Best Day of My Life • Can You Feel the Love Tonight • The Chicken Dance • Do-Re-Mi • Happy Birthday to You • If You're Happy and You Know It • Let It Go • Sing • Star Wars (Main Theme) • Take Me Out to the Ball Game • This Land Is Your Land • Tomorrow • A Whole New World • and more.

00286602 Easy Piano..................................$16.99

SEQUENTIAL POP PIANO SONGS

24 Easy Favorites Carefully Selected and Arranged in Order of Difficulty

All My Loving • Beauty and the Beast • Brave • Daydream Believer • Feel It Still • Hallelujah • Love Me Tender • One Call Away • Over the Rainbow • Perfect • Rolling in the Deep • Shake It Off • Stay with Me • Thinking Out Loud • Unchained Melody • and more.

00279889 Easy Piano..................................$16.99

Disney Characters and Artwork TM & © 2019 Disney
Prices, contents, and availability subject to change without notice.

HAL•LEONARD®
www.halleonard.com